What Really Happened *to* Judas Iscariot?

What Really Happened
to
Judas Iscariot?

Robert E. Daley

The Larry Czerwonka Company
Hilo, Hawai'i

First Edition

Published by: The Larry Czerwonka Company
Printed in the United States of America

ISBN: 0615749321
ISBN-13: 978-0615749327

Contents

What Really Happened *to* Judas Iscariot?

Introduction

This work is **NOT** a defense of, nor a justification for, Judas Iscariot or what he did. However, the story of Judas' role in his ministry with Jesus of Nazareth, and particularly his untimely death, has been formulated and passed on down to us by tradition.

Because of the subject matter, should we take the position that Judas was the spawn of the Devil himself, and should never be considered as a real person? Is he the summation of all that is evil, and as such, his life is unimportant and we should sweep him under the rug and never give a second thought to him?

The Scriptures themselves present to us a very different picture than what we have heard in days gone by, and very possibly for a different reason, which we will attempt to present here. Our prayer is that the reader himself would go to the Word of God to confirm or reject what is put forth in this little work.

Judas Iscariot is a very, very, touchy subject with many people, and disdain many times awaits any individual who would seek to probe deeper into what actually might have happened almost two thousand years ago.

This author's prayer is that all who read this work would be willing to look honestly at the life of any Human Being as someone the Son of God himself came into this Earth to die for.

May all praise ascend to the One who has brought us forth for His good pleasure, and to His Word, which genders truth to all generations.

*** all Bible quotes are from the *King James Version***

The Concept

"His eyes are deep set, beady, and spaced closely together. They are often times bloodshot. His mouth is thin lipped and snarls wryly every time he smiles, saliva dripping from the corners. His posture, slouched, conveys his real character of deceit whenever and wherever he walks. And, an air of darkness hovers over him with his every move."

Is that not the mental picture that many people have of Judas Iscariot? Is he not considered, by Christians, as the epitome of evil? Do we not have our own individual idea of what kind of a person we think Judas was? An idea that has been spawned from all of the stories that we have heard from others during our Christian walk.

Please, do not misunderstand. Judas Iscariot did betray Jesus of Nazareth. He did deliver the Lord of Glory into the hands of sinful men. He is the stated ***"Son of Perdition"*** in the Scriptures. *(John 17:12)* He did submit himself unto Satan. And, in doing these things he did fulfill what the Scriptures prophetically said would come to pass.

And again, this work is **NOT** a defense of him.

But, what was Judas genuinely like as a person? What really did happen to him in those final days just before, and then directly following the crucifixion of Jesus?

The subject of Judas Iscariot has come to the forefront of controversy in recent years. *The Gospel According to Judas* has been put forth, and the idea presented that Judas was instructed to betray Jesus, by Jesus himself. Of course, there is no Scriptural indication of that anywhere. However, the story that has been handed down to us by tradition is not Scripturally sound either. Do we honestly think that we are beyond the reach of Satan or any of his wicked agents? Or, is it possible, concerning the person of Judas Iscariot (and within the context of time) that there, but for the grace of God, possibly go you or I?

May we take the opportunity to examine the Scriptures and follow the course of this man Judas Iscariot and see where they lead. And may the God of all grace and peace guide us as we do, and lead us unto the truth.

The Early Years

It has been written that the name Judas Iscariot is a corruption of *Judas of Kerioth*. And, that Kerioth was a small town a few miles south of Hebron. Hebron is a city in the southern region of Judea, and it would seem that Judas was possibly the only apostle that was not a Galilean. Judas' father's name was Simon *(John 13:2)*.

Did Judas originate from a dysfunctional family? Was he an only child or did he have any brothers or sisters? What kind of child might he have been while growing up? Was he obedient to the Law of Moses? Or was his life one of rebellion from his youth? Did he spend his formative years within the town of his birth, or did he travel elsewhere? Good questions all.

It has been written that, *"The life of Judas is one of unrelieved tragedy. In fact, there is no more tragic spirit in all the world's history. Judas is the greatest failure the world has ever known. His life is a lesson which points vividly to the pitfalls of our spiritual pilgrimage." (The Search for the Twelve Apostles by William Steuart McBirnie, Ph.D.)*

At what point in time did Judas become *"the greatest failure the world has ever known?"* Was it pre-ordained of God from before the foundation of the world? Does God create people like Judas just to fulfill the pages of predestination? To be sure, God did know about him because of foreknowledge. However, was he ever just a *normal* Human Being? Was he simply a pawn in the eternal scheme of things? Was he declared a failure at his birth? If not, how about when he was five years old? No? How about when he became a teenager? At what precise moment in his life did he turn as black as night and as evil as Satan himself?

"And when he had called unto him his twelve disciples, he gave them power against unclean spirits, to cast them out, and to heal all manner of sickness and all manner of disease.

Now the names of the twelve apostles are these: The first, Simon, who is called Peter, and Andrew his brother; James the son of Zebedee, and John his brother;

Philip, and Bartholomew; Thomas, and Matthew the publican; James *the son* of Alphaeus, and Lebbaeus, whose surname was Thaddaeus;

Simon the Canaanite, and Judas Iscariot, who also betrayed him.

These twelve Jesus sent forth, and commanded them, saying . . ." *(Matthew 10:1-5a)*

Our first glimpse of Judas, Scripturally speaking, comes when Jesus calls together men who have been following him for a period of time. On a mountain slope he chooses twelve men, commissions them, and sends them forth.

We will find a similar record in the gospel of Mark 3:14-19, where we shall find that all twelve were ordained for the work that Jesus would send them to do.

In Luke 6:12-16, we find that all those disciples were, at the time of this selection, named Apostles, and that the decision to choose these particular twelve was possibly a result of praying and fasting all-night, and sensitive hearing from the Holy Spirit as to whom would be part of this entourage.

Now, Jesus of Nazareth has spent the last eighteen years of his life saturating himself in the Scriptures as a regular man. He is not operating on this Earth as *God*; he is operating as a Human man, with authority.

He has read the Scriptures, as we all are admonished to do. He has studied the Scriptures as a student of the Word of God. He has memorized the Scriptures that they might virtually become a part of him. He has meditated upon the Scriptures, that the Holy Spirit might bring revelation of truth.

He is knowledgeable of Psalm 41:9 . . .

"Yea, mine own familiar friend, in whom I trusted, which did eat of my bread, hath lifted up *his* heel against me." *(Psalm 41:9)*

However, is this primary Scripture of betrayal, and the excerpt in Psalm 109:6-15 which are the only set of verses of their kind in the whole of the Old Testament, the foremost Scriptures on Jesus' mind when he chooses twelve individuals into whom he is now going to pour himself?

Some of these men are not *first-time* followers of Jesus. Upon his return from the wilderness, Jesus picked up five disciples who witnessed his miracle of turning water into wine at a wedding feast in Cana of Galilee. Those five men left off following Jesus when they all returned to Capernaum. Two of them to unstated endeavors and the other three to their fishing businesses.

After the wedding feast, Jesus ministered, for a period of time, without any disciples at all. He worked miracles and signs and wonders followed him down in Jerusalem, at the feast of Passover, and caught the attention of the religious rulers and the chief priests and the Pharisees without any disciples. *(John 3:23-25)* So, does Jesus, at this time of the selection of the twelve, know who will ultimately hand him over to his enemies?

The Psalm verse above tells us that Judas at one time was a trusted friend of Jesus, and that he and Jesus broke bread together. If, at the time of the selection of those who will closely follow him, Jesus knows that Judas is the betrayer, how will he ever be able to trust him?

What **might** have happened at the outset of this journey? Is it possible that at some point in time Simon Iscariot's son Judas, hears of a man performing miracles and walking in demonstrated authority within the region in which he lives, and purposes to find this man and *check him out?*

Is he the blackness of darkness even now, and purposely sets himself to infiltrate, seduce, deceive, and then betray this man of power? Based on Scriptural evidence, this author does not think so.

Does he have a political motive at this time for following Jesus? Possibly. Does he have an already established agenda even now? Possibly. We don't know because the Scripture does not comment on it. And, unbiblical speculation is unwise.

"And he ordained twelve, that they should be with him, and that he might send them forth to preach,

And to have power to heal sicknesses, and to cast out devils:" *(Mark 3:14-15)*

What we do know is that Judas was one of those chosen by Jesus and that he went out with the other apostles and preached the good news of the Kingdom of God. We know also that Judas was anointed to heal sicknesses and cast out devils. He ate with all of the other apostles, he laughed with all of the other apostles, and he ministered in every aspect, just like all of the other apostles. He observed signs and wonders that were wrought by the power of God through Jesus, and he was fully involved with every area of ministry.

That possibly being the case, then what happened? When and where did Judas begin to go astray? Could it be that when Jesus put together his ministerial team (at the time of the selection of the twelve) governmental positions were immediately established? Is it possible that Judas was, early on, installed as *the keeper of the bag?*

"Then saith one of his disciples, Judas Iscariot, Simon's *son,* which should betray him,

Why was not this ointment sold for three hundred pence, and given to the poor?

This he said, not that he cared for the poor; but because he was a thief, and had the bag, and bare what was put therein." *(John 12:4)*

Entrusted with handling money did Judas' true character begin to seep out shortly after his appointment to the position of treasurer? The Scripture tells us that

"Every man is tempted, when he is drawn away of his own lust and enticed." *(James 1:14)*

What lust within the personage of Judas was Satan able to assault with temptation, and that Judas fell prey to?

"For the love of money is the root of all evil: which while some coveted after, they have erred from the faith, and pierced themselves through with many sorrows." *(I Timothy 6:10)*

Not only does he become a thief, but his heart turns cold toward those who are less fortunate than he.

"For where your treasure is, there will your heart be also." *(Matthew 6:21)*

Has there never been, in all of the days gone by or in this present age, someone who might have followed, or is currently following, this same misguided path?

The fact is that Judas, as a man, made some seriously bad decisions. In whatever form his disobedience might have taken, every decision to sin led him further and further away from God. The Scriptures also tells us that sin hardens the heart. Things haven't changed over the centuries, it is just as true now as it was then.

Jesus of Nazareth did not minister the love and grace of God to the people using his own power. From the time of his return from the wilderness, he ministered to them under the direction of, and by the power of, the gifts of the Holy Spirit that we find recorded in I Corinthians, chapter 12.

Jesus, at the very least, being as sensitive to the Holy Spirit's direction as he was, would have received a Word of Knowledge concerning Judas' activities. This word might have come very early on after the selection of the twelve has already taken place.

"But there are some of you that believe not. For Jesus knew from the beginning who they were that believed not, and who should betray him." *(John 6:64)*

In chapter six of the Gospel of John we see Jesus ministering in the synagogue within the city of Capernaum. It is there that he declares that he is the Bread of Life; and that if one does not eat of his flesh and drink of his blood, then that one has no part with him.

It is also at this time that the above statement is made. Jesus and his apostles have been ministering in various capacities for quite a while. *"From the beginning"* is the key point within this verse. The question becomes *"from the beginning"* of what?

So many times when we look at the person of Jesus of Nazareth within the Scriptures we develop erroneous concepts. Jesus was, and is, God . . . and nothing we may do or say can change that. However, Jesus is also a man. And according to the Scriptures a man who was just like any other man, except without sin.

He was tempted when he was drawn away of his own lusts and enticed, just like we are. And yes, Jesus of Nazareth did have lusts. He got hungry just like we do. He became fatigued just like we do. He became angry just as we do. There were things that he did not want to do, just like we have things that we do not want to do. And he used the restroom just like we have to.

What Jesus did <u>not</u> do is read somebody's mind. Men cannot read minds. And Jesus, as a man, is no different. He did not automatically know things. What we have in Jesus is a Human Being without sin attached to his personage. He does not think bad thoughts, he does not say bad words, and he does not do bad things. He has no sin.

And what he is doing in ministry, he is doing by the power of the Holy Spirit. The purpose behind this is: that it was the Holy Spirit of God that did all the ministerial work through Jesus ... so when the time comes it will be the same Holy Spirit of God doing all the ministerial work through you and me. Jesus then, is only going to know about any particular individual what the Holy Spirit will reveal to him.

That being the case, **". . . Jesus knew from the beginning who they were that believed not, and who should betray him."** *(John 6:64)*

When did the Holy Spirit reveal to Jesus the true character of Judas? At what point in time did Jesus actually know that Judas Iscariot was the friend that would lift up his heel against him? And Scripture has no comment on that other than **"from the beginning."**

This author believes that the insight as to whom the traitor was, came to Jesus from the Holy Spirit; and that this word was not given at the time of Jesus choosing the twelve, but may have been given as the corrupted character behavior of Judas began to become more pronounced.

"Then Simon Peter answered him, Lord, to whom shall we go? thou hast the words of eternal life.

And we believe and are sure that thou art that Christ, the Son of the living God.

Jesus answered them, Have not I chosen you twelve, and one of you is a devil?

He spake of Judas Iscariot *the son* of Simon: for he it was that should betray him, being one of the twelve." *(John 6:68-71)*

At this particular point in real time then, Jesus knows that Judas Iscariot is, in fact, the traitor and refers to him as a devil. This particular Scriptural reference clearly reflects character. We saw in John 12:6 that Judas had become a thief. Character corrupted. It may be that after moving into a ministerial position Judas witnesses how smoothly Jesus works with the Holy Spirit. Possibly because Jesus is so trusting, Judas found an avenue to begin to siphon off funds without anyone seemingly knowing.

In addition to Judas, we have in the Scriptures, another example of a person that genuinely knew Jesus and yet his heart was not right:

"Then Simon himself believed also: and when he was baptized, he continued with Philip, and wondered, beholding the miracles and signs which were done."

"And when Simon saw that through laying on of the apostles' hands the Holy Ghost was given, he offered them money,

Saying, Give me also this power, that on whomsoever I lay hands, he may receive the Holy Ghost.

But Peter said unto him, Thy money perish with thee, because thou hast thought that the gift of God may be purchased with money.

Thou hast neither part nor lot in this matter: for thy heart is not right in the sight of God." *(Acts 8:13, 18-21)*

Simon's **heart** was not right in the sight of God. Yet, Simon was *Born-Again*. He was a New Creation in Christ Jesus; however, his **heart** was not right.

Understand that no one walking during the days that Judas walked with Jesus was *Born-Again*. No one was a recreated, Holy Spirit empowered new species of Human Being. So, if someone who has become a New Creation can have a **heart** that is not right in the sight of God ... might it also be possible that an unredeemed man, even though he is physically walking with Jesus, would have a **heart** that is not right, in the sight of God?

Thus, Judas is a perfect candidate for Satan to tempt, and pressure, and utilize to fulfill his plan.

The Betrayal

Leading up to the betrayal is the crescendo of Jesus' rising popularity with the average individual, and the rising hatred against him from those whom he challenged with truth.

Jesus' raising Lazarus from the dead was, as it were, the straw that broke the camel's back. At this point in time his opponents may have determined that if he is able to raise people from the dead, there is no stopping him. Something must be done. However, they feared the people because the people received Jesus as a prophet come from God. Somehow this must be done privately.

Several days before the feast of the Passover, after Jesus and the apostles have returned unto Jerusalem, a fortuitous event seems to have occurred for the chief priests.

"Then one of the twelve, called Judas Iscariot, went unto the chief priests.

And said *unto* them, What will ye give me, and I will deliver him unto you? And they covenanted with him for thirty pieces of silver.

And from that time he sought opportunity to betray him." *(Matthew 26:14-16)*

"And Judas Iscariot, one of the twelve, went unto the chief priests, to betray him unto them.

And when they heard *it,* they were glad, and promised to give him money. And he sought how he might conveniently betray him." *(Mark 14:10-11)*

"Then entered Satan into Judas surnamed Iscariot, being of the number of the twelve.

And he went his way, and communed with the chief priests and captains, how he might betray him unto them.

And they were glad, and covenanted to give him money.

And he promised, and sought opportunity to betray him unto them in the absence of the multitude." *(Luke 22:3-6)*

At this point in time, many believe that Judas, being politically motivated, agreed to betray Jesus to the chief priests in order to force his hand. The idea being that if Jesus were actually arrested by his enemies he would rise up under that pressure, in righteous indignation and use his power to free himself and then be able to go on to free the Nation of Israel from the Roman occupation.

Please remember that at the time, the individuals who were involved in these events were not spiritually minded. They were carnal men, and the Messiah that they were expecting was one who would free them from the Roman yoke of occupation and bondage. Jesus was not moving in that direction, which might be why Judas, some would say, would try and force his hand.

However, we also see that Judas' corrupted character is showing again. He is a man of thorny ground, and has become a prisoner of the *"deceitfulness of riches"* and a lover of mammon *(Mark 4:19)*. Even though Jesus has provided for everything that any of the apostles needed or could want, for Judas, it is not enough. He is an ideal example of the Scripture:

"But they that will be rich fall into temptation and a snare, and *into* many foolish and hurtful lusts, which drown men in destruction and perdition.

For the love of money is the root of all evil: which while some coveted after, they have erred from the faith, and pierced themselves through with many sorrows." *(I Timothy 6:9-10)*

That being said, the groundwork is now laid. The Scripture tells us that Judas now looked for a *convenient* way in which he might deliver Jesus into their hands.

Several days later that *convenient* way might be coming available.

"Now before the feast of the Passover, when Jesus knew that his hour was come that he should depart out of this world unto the Father, having loved his own which were in the world, he loved them unto the end.

And supper being ended, the devil having now put into the heart of Judas Iscariot, Simon's *son,* to betray him;" *(John 13:1-2)*

We are now at the Last Supper in real time. This is not the first time that Jesus and his disciples have ever been in Jerusalem. Nor is this the first time that Jesus and his disciples have eaten a dinner together while in Jerusalem. The Scripture says that Jesus often times resorted to the Garden of Gethsemane when he was in that city.

"This will be perfect!" might be a thought that would be presented to Judas by Satan. This could be the **convenient** way that he was looking for. And Judas receiving that thought locks himself into the skewed thinking that is going on within him. An example of just one of the many bad decisions that Judas made which ultimately marked him to become the *"son of perdition."* *(John 17:12)*

"For he knew who should betray him; therefore said he, Ye are not all clean.

So after he had washed their feet, and was set down again, he said unto them, Know ye what I have done to you?

Ye call me Master and Lord: and ye say well; for so I am.

If I then, *your* Lord and Master, have washed your feet; ye also ought to wash one another's feet.

For I have given you an example, that ye should do as I have done to you.

Verily, verily, I say unto you, The servant is not greater than his lord; neither he that is sent greater than he that sent him.

If ye know these things, happy are ye if ye do them.

I speak not of you all: I know whom I have chosen: but that the scripture may be fulfilled, He that eateth bread with me lifted up his heel against me.

Now I tell you before it come, that, when it is come to pass, ye may believe that I am *he*." *(John 13:11-19)*

Here at the Last Supper Jesus is speaking clearly, and even referencing the Scriptures, but his disciples, and particularly Judas, are not hearing him.

"When Jesus had thus said, he was troubled in spirit, and testified, and said, Verily, verily, I say unto you, that one of you shall betray me.

Then the disciples looked on one another, doubting of whom he spake.

Now there was leaning on Jesus' bosom one of his disciples, whom Jesus loved.

Simon Peter therefore beckoned to him, that he should ask who it should be of whom he spake.

He then lying on Jesus' breast saith unto him, Lord, who is it?

Jesus answered, He it is, to whom I shall give a sop, when I have dipped *it*. And when he had dipped the sop, he gave *it* to Judas Iscariot, *the son* of Simon.

And after the sop Satan entered into him. Then said Jesus unto him, That thou doest, do quickly." *(John 13:21-27)*

"And as they did eat, he said, Verily I say unto you, that one of you shall betray me.

And they were exceeding sorrowful, and began every one of them to say unto him, Lord, is it I?

And he answered and said, He that dippeth *his* hand with me in the dish, the same shall betray me.

The Son of man goeth as it is written of him: but woe unto that man by whom the Son of man is betrayed! it had been good for that man if he had not been born.

Then Judas which betrayed him, answered and said, Master, is it I? He said unto him, Thou hast said." *(Matthew 26:21-25)*

These two Scripture excerpts give us the details of the moments leading up to the actual betrayal itself. Jesus is *"troubled in spirit"* as he is about to make the announcement that one of those sitting at the table with him is going to betray him.

This author believes that Jesus was troubled, not because of what was going to happen to him personally, but rather because of what was going to happen to Judas Eternally.

"woe unto that man" . . . **"it had been good for that man if he had not been born."** *(Matthew 26:24)*

These are severe and weighty statements to make. Jesus is actually giving Judas an opportunity to change his mind by potentially giving insight into the consequences of his bad decisions.

Many people believe that Judas honestly had no choice in the matter. The Scripture had foretold of him, and there is nothing that he could do about it. That is just not so. Even though it is written:

"Set thou a wicked man over him: and let Satan stand at his right hand.

When he shall be judged, let him be condemned: and let his prayer become sin.

Let his days be few; *and* **let another take his office.**

Let his children be fatherless, and his wife a widow.

Let his children be continually vagabonds, and beg: let them seek *their bread* **also out of their desolate places.**

Let the extortioner catch all that he hath; and let the strangers spoil his labour.

Let there be none to extend mercy unto him: neither let there be any to favour his fatherless children.

Let his posterity be cut off; *and* **in the generation following let their name be blotted out.**

Let the iniquity of his fathers be remembered with the Lord; and let not the sin of his mother be blotted out.

Let them be before the Lord continually, that he may cut off the memory of them from the earth." *(Psalm 109:6-15)*

A segment of Scripture, to be sure, which details the dreadful consequences of the betrayer and his family, for what he will do. Nevertheless, Judas Iscariot is not named here in these verses.

The Scripture will surely be fulfilled ... but every free-willed, intelligent, moral Human Being always has a choice. The Scriptures tell us that God is not willing that **"ANY should perish"** *(II Peter 3:9)*, and that statement includes Judas. However, foreknowledge has also cast the Scriptural die concerning the free-will bad decisions that Judas would make.

We have the opportunity, in the days in which we live, to make just as many bad decisions as Judas did. No one is forcing us. And, in spite of what Scripture says, in spite of our God giving us insight into the consequences of our sinful decisions, there are many, even those who are called "Christians" that will disregard the warnings and ultimately find themselves in the same abode of torment that Judas now occupies.

Also, within these excerpts, and within the Gospel of Luke, it is stated that **'Satan entered into him"** *(Luke 22:3)*. Please understand that Satan is an angel occupying his own celestial body. He **cannot** enter into, and possess a human being. He can influence a human being through thought, and apply pressure to that person's free-will. He can also direct a disembodied spirit, a demon, to enter into and possess a person . . . if that person is willing to let that spirit in. But without interior demonic possession he cannot directly make a person do anything that they do not choose to do.

"And when they had sung an hymn, they went out into the mount of Olives." *(Mark 14:26)*

The supper is now ended and Jesus has directed the disciples to the Garden of Gethsemane for a time of prayer.

We are familiar with the story of Jesus separating himself from most of the disciples and taking Peter, James, and John for support while he anguished in prayer. His petition to his heavenly Father, **". . . take away this cup from me: nevertheless not what I will, but what thou wilt"** *(Mark 14:36)*. This statement is a glimpse into the humanity side of Jesus. Spiritually speaking, he knew for what purpose he had come. And, though he dreaded what lay ahead, he again demonstrated obedience and yieldedness to the Holy Spirit.

Having obtained victory in the spirit, by the power of the Holy Spirit, Jesus is now ready to endure the heinous physical death that lay directly ahead.

"Rise up, let us go; lo, he that betrayeth me is at hand.

And immediately, while he yet spake, cometh Judas, one of the twelve, and with him a great multitude with swords and staves, from the chief priests and the scribes and the elders.

And he that betrayeth him had given them a token, saying, Whomsoever I shall kiss, that same is he; take him, and lead *him* **away safely.**

And as soon as he was come, he goeth straightway to him, and saith, Master, master; and kissed him.

And they laid their hands on him, and took him."
(Mark 14:42-46)

"And while he yet spake, behold a multitude, and he that was called Judas, one of the twelve, went before them, and drew near unto Jesus to kiss him.

But Jesus said unto him, Judas, betrayest thou the Son of man with a kiss?" *(Luke 22:47-48)*

"And Judas also, which betrayed him, knew the place: for Jesus oftimes resorted thither with his disciples.

Judas then, having received a band *of men* and officers from the chief priests and Pharisees, cometh thither with lanterns and torches and weapons." *(John 18:2-3)*

These Scriptures are the nucleus of the betrayal. This is the pinnacle of Judas' scheme. Opportunity has presented itself, that in a *convenient* manner Judas has been able to deliver to the chief priests his Master, Jesus. Now Jesus will be caught in a pincer move and he will have to demonstrate his power to free himself, and then we can move on to confront the Romans. Judas may have been giddy with the thought of how he was able to maneuver Jesus into the hands of the religious hierarchy.

However, please note: if Judas is so scurrilous and evil, why in the Gospel of Mark do we find him saying **"lead *him* away safely"**? *(Mark 14:44)* Why should Judas care whether or not they treat Jesus safely or in a rough manner?

Yes, he has betrayed Jesus . . . Yes, he probably does have a political agenda at this time . . . And, yes, he was able to benefit financially from this action. However, Judas' concern for the soldiers to deal with Jesus safely shows that he is not totally sold out to darkness at this point.

"Jesus saith unto him, Thou hast said: nevertheless I say unto you, Hereafter shall ye see the Son of man sitting on the right hand of power, and coming in the clouds of heaven.

Then the high priest rent his clothes, saying, He hath spoken blasphemy; what further need have we of witnesses? behold, now ye have heard his blasphemy.

What think ye? They answered and said, He is guilty of death." *(Matthew 26:64-66)*

After being arrested Jesus is taken to stand before the high priest, and then stand before Pontius Pilate, and then stand before Herod the King, and then return again to the seat of Pontius Pilate. He has been kept up all night. He is now about to be scourged. And, word reaches Judas that Jesus has been condemned.

"Then Judas, which had betrayed him, when he saw that he was condemned, repented himself, and brought again the thirty pieces of silver to the chief priests and elders,

Saying, I have sinned in that I have betrayed the innocent blood. And they said, What *is that* to us? see thou *to that.*

And he cast down the pieces of silver in the temple, and departed." *(Matthew 27:3-5)*

Whoa! What is this? Judas **"repented himself"**? He **"brought again the thirty pieces of silver"**? He said, **"I have sinned in that I have betrayed the innocent blood"**?

This does not sound like the Judas that this author was told about when he became a Christian. This author does not picture a man with deep set, beady, closely spaced, bloodshot eyes when he reads these verses. He does indeed picture a man who has made a particularly bad decision, erred greatly, and has come to recognize his mistake, and moves to undo his previous actions. Or, should we just dismiss these statements and ignore these records that the Spirit of Truth has given unto us?

And this is **NOT** a defense of Judas' actions. But it is an observation based upon the information that is given to us in Scripture.

This author, based upon the testimony of Scripture, believes that Judas was a regular man, just like you or me. This author believes that Judas was drawn to the charisma of Jesus of Nazareth, just like hundreds of thousands of others in this world.

This author believes that Judas made some very bad decisions, just like millions of other people have. This author also believes, because of the Scriptural record, that Judas repented and was sorry for what he had done. Not necessarily because he had fully come to his senses, but because his maneuver to force Jesus' hand did not at all work. Jesus is not going to use his power to deliver himself and oppose the Romans, but rather is now condemned to death. Judas now recognizes this, and that **may** be at least one of the reasons that he is now sorry for what he has done.

* * *

And here is where tradition has told us that Judas went out IMMEDIATELY and hanged himself.

Now, part of this problem is that the punctuation in Matthew 27:5 is incorrect. Punctuation is not Divinely inspired. There should be a period, not a comma, after the word **"departed"** in this verse. Judas' actions that took place within the temple end with his departing from the temple. And, at some point in time, Judas did hang himself. However, it was not something that occurred immediately.

Three Days and Three Nights

In order to fully understand the story of Judas Iscariot, we must have clarity of what happened during the next four days and three nights.

Satan has successfully seduced a Human man to be an unprecedented stooge for hell. Through this man, Satan has delivered the one Human Being that has withstood and defeated him at every turn, into the hands of his own active Human agents here on this earth. At this point in real time, the kingdom of darkness is thrilled!

"And when Jesus had cried with a loud voice, he said, Father, into thy hands I commend my spirit: and having said thus, he gave up the ghost." *(Luke 23:46)*

Jesus then, has been crucified. The Scriptures declare, and Jesus himself said that he would be in the tomb for three days and three nights.

In order to confirm the truth of this doctrine it is necessary to count backward from the Scriptural anchor day, the Sabbath of Commandment.

"Six days shall work be done: but the seventh day *is* the sabbath of rest, an holy convocation; ye shall do no work *therein:* it *is* the sabbath of the Lord in all your dwellings." *(Leviticus 23:3)*

That is the day of the week that we all know of as Saturday.

"This man *(Joseph of Arimathaea)* **went unto Pilate, and begged the body of Jesus.**

And he took it down, and wrapped it in linen, and laid it in a sepulchre that was hewn in stone, wherein never man before was laid.

And that day was the preparation, and the sabbath drew on.

And the women also which came with him from Galilee, followed after, and beheld the sepulchre, and how his body was laid.

And they returned, and prepared spices and ointments; and rested the sabbath day according to the commandment." *(Luke 23:52-56)*

We see here in Luke that Joseph of Arimathaea came to Pontius Pilate after Jesus was declared dead, probably in the later part of the day, and begged for Jesus' body to be released to him. Joseph, Nicodemus, and possibly some servants, then took the body off of the cross, slathered it with about a hundred pounds of aloes, wrapped it in burial linen, and laid the body in a nearby sepulchre because of time constraints.

The women watching the process performed by the two Pharisees, purpose to return, at the first opportunity and properly prepare the body for a prophet's final burial.

Here, in Luke, the women **"prepared spices and ointments"** and then rested on Saturday, the Sabbath of Commandment. That means that they prepared these spices on a Friday.

"And when the sabbath was past, Mary Magdalene, and Mary the *mother* of James, and Salome, had bought sweet spices, that they might come and anoint him." *(Mark 16:1)*

This verse in Mark denotes that **"the sabbath was past"**. So, the **"sabbath** that **was past"** is not the Sabbath of Commandment, which is Saturday, but rather another sabbath, one of the **"Feasts of the Lord"** that we find in the book of Leviticus chapter 23.

"The Jews therefore, because it was the preparation, that the bodies should not remain upon the cross on the sabbath day, (for that sabbath day was a high day), besought Pilate that their legs might be broken, and *that* they might be taken away." *(John 19:31)*

So . . . to save time and abbreviate what undoubtedly took place:
* Jesus was arrested on a Tuesday evening.
* He was shuffled back and forth all Tuesday night to the various 'kangaroo courts' that he was tried at.

* He was crucified on a Wednesday morning at 9:00 a.m. and hangs on the cross for six hours.

* He dies on Wednesday afternoon at 3:00 p.m. of a broken heart over those he loves.

* He is placed within the sepulchre just before 6:00 p.m. on Wednesday, which is the preparation day for the 'high day' sabbath, because there can be no working after 6:00 p.m.

In the year that Jesus was crucified, the Passover feast occurred on a Thursday. No work of any kind can be done on that day. However, the Pharisees that hated Jesus did go to Pilate on that **"high day"** *(John 19:31)* and persuaded him to give them a guard to seal and watch the tomb.

Friday is a day that the women can, and do, go shopping at the market for the spices and ointments that they needed to anoint the body of Jesus.

Friday is also the day that they prepare those spices, but not in time to go to the sepulchre and deal with the body properly.

The Sabbath of Commandment is the next day, and again no work can be done on that day.

The earliest opportunity that the women have to complete the necessary task is on Sunday, as early as possible . . . because Jesus will have been in the grave for four days and just like Lazarus, he will stink.

The three *"night"* periods then, were Wednesday night, Thursday night, and Friday night, according to how we calculate them in line with the Roman calendar.

The three *"day"* periods were Thurs-day, Fri-day, and Satur-day.

Jesus was **NOT** crucified on a Friday as has been passed down to us by tradition. He was arrested on a Tuesday evening and shuffled around to the High Priest, Pilate, and king Herod all night long. Being returned to Pilate he is scourged, and Pilate then desires to set him free. The fervor of the religious rulers compels him to execute Jesus, and his body lies in the tomb for three nights and three days.

Jesus himself is in the Sheol/Hades compartment of the *Nether World*, paying the price that Sin demands, for the whole world.

A study of the Scriptures will reveal that on Saturday, the Sabbath of Commandment, just before 6:00 p.m., Jesus is raised up from the dead. A Sunday resurrection would have put him into the fourth day and would violate Scriptural records.

Resurrection Morning

Scripture declares that Jesus—**"preached to the spirits in prison."**
(I Peter 3:19)

And Jesus being then loosed from—**"the pains of death: because it was not possible that he should be holden of it"** *(Acts 2:24)*

He goes into the abode of Paradise or Abraham's Bosom and presents himself as the promised Messiah to the few men that had called upon the name of the Lord before the days of Noah, and to the covenant Jewish people who believed on what God had declared. He is The One that John the Baptist has been talking about, to all those who have died in faith, believing on God's promises, from the time of Adam.

Being now resurrected, when he leaves the *Nether World* he leads **"captivity captive"** *(Eph. 4:8)* and empties the Paradise compartment of its inhabitants.

Some of those inhabitants from Paradise, according to the Word of God — **"went into the holy city, and appeared unto many."** *(Matthew 27:53)*

This is the chronology of what took place **after** his resurrection:

* On Sunday, the first day of the week, during the dark of the night, the stone is rolled away by—**"the angel of the Lord."** *(Matthew 28:2)* And the tomb lay open to any and all.

* Mary Magdalene and the other women go to the tomb to anoint and re-wrap the body of Jesus, wondering who will help them with the stone. Very early on that Sunday morning they arrive at the grave site, and find the stone already rolled away and the tomb empty.

Jesus is already resurrected but has not yet stepped outside of the sepulchre onto this earth again. At this point in time, he is involved with other things.

While inside the tomb, holy angels appear to them and instruct them to tell Jesus' disciples to go into Galilee and—**"there shall ye see him."** *(Mark 16:7)*

* While in Jerusalem, the disciples are not all staying together in one place. At the sepulchre the angel directs the women to

". . . go your way, tell his disciples and Peter that he goeth before you into Galilee:" *(Mark 16:7)*

* Mary knows where Peter is, and the other women go to tell the rest of the disciples what the angels have declared.

* Mary goes to the house where Peter, John, Cleopas, and possibly Luke are staying. She reports what she has seen and heard from the angels. Peter quickly awakes, and from this news dresses hurriedly. *(Luke 24:22-23)*

"Peter therefore went forth, and that other disciple, and came to the sepulchre." *(John 20:3)*

* He and John find the tomb empty when they arrive, as Mary has said. After their investigation

"Then the disciples went away again unto their own home." *(John 20:10)*

* They are puzzled, and do not honestly know what has happened.

* Mary returns to the grave site and enters the tomb again. She has a second angelic visitation, and encounters Jesus as she begins to leave the sepulchre. Jesus tenderly gives her instructions to avoid him being defiled:

"Touch me not; for I am not yet ascended to my Father: but go to my brethren, and say unto them, I ascend unto my Father, and your Father; and *to* my God and your God." *(John 20:17)*

* Mary leaves to obey Jesus' command and Jesus then ascends into heaven at an incalculable speed and presents his blood upon the Mercy Seat, within the True Tabernacle.

"For Christ is not entered into the holy places made with hands, *which are* the figures of the true; but into heaven itself, now to appear in the presence of God for us:

Nor yet that he should offer himself often, as the priest entereth into the holy place every year with blood of others;

For then must he often have suffered since the foundation of the world: but now once in the end of the world hath he appeared to put away sin by the sacrifice of himself."
(Hebrews 9:24-26)

* Returning from heaven at an incalculable speed Jesus now has no blood within his resurrected, glorified, Spiritual body. There is nothing to be defiled by touch, so the women, still on their way to inform the disciples, can lay their hands upon his feet when he appears with the greeting **"All hail."** *(Matt. 28:9-10)*

* Reports begin to reach the ears of the disciples that Jesus is raised from the dead. The *other women* tell the gathered apostles that they have seen Jesus. Mary Magdalene tells the gathered apostles that she has seen him, and the two followers of Jesus who went to Emmaus tell the gathered apostles that Jesus is alive. And in spite of all of these reports the disciples don't believe any of them. *(Luke 24:9-11; Mark 16:10-13; John 20:18)*

The Testimony of Scripture

The events that we have just touched upon in the previous chapter are mostly familiar to all of us. Some of the details are not usually brought out, but the basic knowledge of what happened is told again and again.

Many times the testimony of the four eye witness accounts of the resurrected Christ are read, and yet not thoroughly understood.

"And returned from the sepulchre, and told all these things unto THE ELEVEN, and to all the rest.

It was Mary Magdalene, and Joanna, and Mary *the mother* of James, and other *women that were* with them, which told these things unto the apostles.

And their words seemed to them as idle tales, and they believed them not." *(Luke 24:9-11)*

This first record that we have actually incorporates two testimony accounts. The testimony of Mary Magdalenes's account is found in the Gospel of John. John clearly shows that, at a given time, only Peter, John, and Mary Magdalene were at the sepulchre. After Mary receives instructions from Jesus himself, she returns, by herself, to where the other disciples are and relays what she has seen and heard.

The second account that we have originates from Matthew 28:9-10. And there, in the account in Matthew, after Jesus gives instructions to these *other women*, some of which are named in Luke 24:10, they also come to the grieving disciples and report that they have indeed seen and heard the Lord.

And please note that the Scripture states that these reports were given to ELEVEN disciples.

"And they rose up the same hour, and returned to Jerusalem, and found THE ELEVEN gathered together, and them that were with them.

Saying, The Lord is risen indeed, and hath appeared to Simon." *(Luke 24:33-34)*

The second record that we have from Luke also incorporates two eye witness accounts. The first testimony comes from the two travelers on the road to Emmaus.

They report that they have seen and heard the Lord Jesus. However, they also report that at some point in time Jesus has appeared to Simon Peter, which is the second eye witness account.

Again, note that the Scripture states that these reports were given to ELEVEN disciples.

"Afterward he appeared unto THE ELEVEN as they sat at meat, and upbraided them with their unbelief and hardness of heart, because they believed not them which had seen him after he was risen." *(Mark 16:14)*

This third account is one of Jesus himself actually appearing to the ELEVEN as they were having supper that evening. At this occasion we see that Jesus scolds the disciples for their refusal to receive the reports that were given unto them by the *other women*, by Mary Magdalene, by Peter, and by the two from the Emmaus journey, concerning his resurrection.

However, there is also another very powerful notation that we need to consider:

"But Thomas, one of the twelve, call Didymus, was NOT WITH THEM when Jesus came." *(John 20:24)*

Throughout the entire Resurrection Day proceedings of these various eye witness accounts; and the subsequent first appearance of Jesus that evening to eleven of his chosen twelve, Thomas is **NOT** found to be around.

Thomas is not there when Mary Magdalene comes to testify. Thomas is not there when the *other women* come to testify. Thomas is not there when Peter joins the other disciples and testifies that Jesus has appeared unto him. And, Thomas is not there on that Resurrection Day evening, at supper time, when Jesus himself appears to scold his disciples for unbelief.

The Gospel of Luke tells us twice that these reports were made to ELEVEN disciples. In Mark's gospel Jesus appears to ELEVEN disciples and scolds them for not believing the reports they received.

And in John's gospel we find out that Thomas was **NOT** with the other disciples at this first appearance of Jesus since his resurrection.

Again, tradition has told us that Judas went right out, after he returned the pieces of silver, and killed himself. But the Scriptures tell us of **ELEVEN** disciples receiving reports of his resurrection. And, that Thomas was **NOT** one of them.

In addition, later on the apostle Paul will tell us, under the anointing of the Holy Spirit of Truth, that Jesus appeared to all **TWELVE** disciples after he was raised from the dead. *(I Corinthians 15:5)* And this is not something that took place after the selection of Matthias. The only plausible explanation, even though it goes completely against what tradition has passed down, is that **JUDAS ISCARIOT IS STILL ALIVE!**

And if that is the case, that means that Judas Iscariot lived through Jesus' crucifixion . . . the reports of so many witnesses . . . Jesus himself actually appearing and speaking to his disciples . . . and Thomas's doubting.

Scripture also reveals,

"The same day at evening, being the first *day* of the week, when the doors were shut where the disciples were assembled for fear of the Jews, came Jesus and stood in the midst, and saith unto them, Peace *be* unto you,

And when he had so said, he showed unto them *his* hands and his side. Then were the disciples glad, when they saw the Lord.

Then said Jesus to them again, Peace *be* unto you: as *my* Father hath sent me, even so send I you.

And when he had said this, he <u>breathed on *them*</u>, and saith unto them, Receive ye the Holy Ghost:

Whosoever sins ye remit, they are remitted unto them; *and* whosoever *sins* ye retain, they are retained." *(John 20:19-23)*

This particular excerpt in Scripture is **very** significant because this is where the *Church* began, **NOT** on the Day of Pentecost. This is where the disciples of Jesus were *Born-Again.*

The Holy Spirit, according to Jesus is
"The Spirit of truth whom the world cannot receive, because it seeth him not, neither knoweth him: but ye know him; for he dwelleth with you, and shall be in you." *(John 14:17)*

If Jesus **"breathed on *them,* and saith unto them, Receive ye the Holy Ghost:"** *(John 20:22)* . . . then they received the Holy Ghost. And this *__initiating__* act of Jesus is the first occasion of men being *Born-Again.*

Since this action occurred with ELEVEN disciples on the evening of Resurrection Day, and Thomas was not with them, then Judas Iscariot was one of those disciples who were *Born-Again* on that evening.

Now this author knows that this kind of statement is going to infuriate many people. So . . . in all fairness, if this is just not so ... if this is just preposterous, then SCRIPTURALLY, DISPROVE IT! Not opinion—that is worth nothing. Not emotion—that is worth nothing. Not tradition — that is the one thing that makes the Word of God of **"none effect"** *(Matthew 15:6)*. Take the Scriptures and build a case in opposition to what has just been presented.

And, this author is not attempting to be contentious. He is just interested in the TRUTH.

In the Scriptures it is revealed that, at various times, Jesus prayed specifically for certain people. He prayed for the eleven disciples after Judas had left the Last Supper to betray him *(John 17:6-17)*. He prayed for Peter after Satan tried to sift him. *(Luke 22:31-32)*. And, he prayed for you and me in his prayers recorded by the apostle John *(John 17:20-24)*.

However, **Jesus NEVER prayed for Judas Iscariot.** In fact, if Jesus had prayed for Judas he would be doing something contrary to the Scriptures. They speak about the **"friend who would lift up his heel against me,"** *(Psalms 41:9)* the one who would betray the Lord of Glory. Jesus even declares that he has lost none of those whom the Father has given him except Judas, **"that the Scripture might be fulfilled"** *(John 17:12)*.

Because the book of James declares to us "the effectual fervent prayer of a righteous man availeth much" *(James 5:16)* this author believes that the prayers of Jesus have strengthened and sustained Peter, the disciples, and you and me against the attacks of the Wicked One. But, not so for Judas.

This author also purports, that because Jesus **could not** and **did not** pray for Judas, that after the resurrection:

* even though Judas was *Born-Again* . . .

* even though Judas was in fellowship with the other
disciples . . .

* even though Jesus himself was in the midst . . .

* even though Judas was there when Thomas
declared **"my Lord and my God"** *(John 20:28)* . . . Satan still was able to accuse, condemn, and overwhelm Judas with overmuch sorrow. Because of that, Judas had no protection against the fiery darts and was driven to the point of suicide.

Sadly, Satan is still able to prevail against many in his assaults. However, it is crucial for us to remember that Judas Iscariot was numbered amongst the twelve, **"and had obtained part of this ministry"** *(Acts 1:17)*. He was empowered by Jesus to heal the sick and cast out devils. He heard and even walked with the living Word of God.

He did betray the Lord of Glory. He did yield to Satan's subtleties. Jesus did say **"Have not I chosen you twelve, and one of you is a devil"** *(John 6:70)*.

But—did Judas know that he was a devil? Did he purpose to be, and to act like, a devil? Even while he was healing the sick and casting out devils? Or—was he a man like you and me, who made a series of very bad decisions, particularly at the end. His nature, like ours, was flawed by sin. However, he chose not to gird up the loins of his mind.

This author believes that the God of all creation is a God of love, and not a creator of evil. Because He is, and because of free will, things could have been different. But, He is also a God who knows and declares **"the end from the beginning"** *(Isaiah 46:10)*. And, because of that . . . because of foreknowledge, they weren't.

This will not be a popular work. Much emotion and animosity will be gendered by what is presented here. And, that is very sad. We live in an age where men are not terribly interested in the truth.

May the God of all grace be merciful unto us. The end is near.

Meet the Author

By-The-Book Ministries, Inc. began in 2001 as a teaching outreach. Rob E. Daley has been gifted by God to be able to explain biblical truths in an easy to understand manner.

Many have been blessed by his teaching style.

Rob was saved and filled with the Holy Spirit in 1978 and has been instructed by the greatest teacher of all—the Spirit of Truth Himself. Rob is an ordained minister with the Assemblies of God International Fellowship and has pastored in various churches over the past 34 years.

It is the desire of this ministry to see the body of Christ solidly taught, and grow up into the things of the Lord. Rob is available for seminars, retreats, conventions, etc.

Rob can be reached at:

thedaleys@bythebookministries.org

http://robdaleyauthor.com

www.ingramcontent.com/pod-product-compliance
Lightning Source LLC
Chambersburg PA
CBHW072041060426
42449CB00010BA/2384